INTO Wild Borneo

BLACKBIRCH®
PRESS

THOMSON
★
™
GALE

San Diego • Detroit • New York • San Francisco • Cleveland • New Haven, Conn. • Waterville, Maine • London • Munich

LIBRARY OF CONGRESS CATALOGING-IN-PUBLICATION DATA

Into wild Borneo / Elaine Pascoe, book editor.
    p. cm. — (The Jeff Corwin experience)
Based on an episode from a Discovery Channel program hosted by Jeff Corwin.
Summary: Television personality Jeff Corwin takes the reader on an expedition through the jungles of Borneo, and introduces some of the diverse wildife found there.
Includes bibliographical references and index.
 ISBN 1-56711-859-3 (hardback : alk. paper) — ISBN 1-4103-0170-2 (paperback : alk. paper)
 1. Zoology—Borneo—Juvenile literature. [1. Zoology—Borneo. 2. Borneo—Description and travel. 3. Corwin, Jeff.] I. Pascoe, Elaine. II. Corwin, Jeff. III. Series.

 QL319.5.I58 2004
 591.9598'3—dc21   2003009283

Printed in China
10 9 8 7 6 5 4 3 2 1

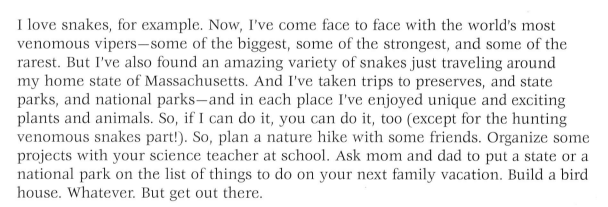

Ever since I was a kid, I dreamed about traveling around the world, visiting exotic places, and seeing all kinds of incredible animals. And now, guess what? That's exactly what I get to do!

Yes, I am incredibly lucky. But, you don't have to have your own television show on Animal Planet to go off and explore the natural world around you. I mean, I travel to Madagascar and the Amazon and all kinds of really cool places—but I don't need to go that far to see amazing wildlife up close. In fact, I can find thousands of incredible critters right here, in my own backyard—or in my neighbor's yard (he does get kind of upset when he finds me crawling around in the bushes, though). The point is, no matter where you are, there's fantastic stuff to see in nature. All you have to do is look.

I love snakes, for example. Now, I've come face to face with the world's most venomous vipers—some of the biggest, some of the strongest, and some of the rarest. But I've also found an amazing variety of snakes just traveling around my home state of Massachusetts. And I've taken trips to preserves, and state parks, and national parks—and in each place I've enjoyed unique and exciting plants and animals. So, if I can do it, you can do it, too (except for the hunting venomous snakes part!). So, plan a nature hike with some friends. Organize some projects with your science teacher at school. Ask mom and dad to put a state or a national park on the list of things to do on your next family vacation. Build a bird house. Whatever. But get out there.

As you read through these pages and look at the photos, you'll probably see how jazzed I get when I come face to face with beautiful animals. That's good. I want you to feel that excitement. And I want you to remember that—even if you don't have your own TV show—you can still experience the awesome beauty of nature almost anywhere you go—any day of the week. I only hope that I can help bring that awesome power and beauty a little closer to you. Enjoy!

Best Wishes!
Jeff

INTO
Wild Borneo

Flying frogs, pythons, the rare proboscis monkey, orangutans—all those creatures are here. It's just a matter of finding them. The third largest island on the planet, Borneo straddles the equator in the South China Sea. Our mission here is to discover as many animals as possible.

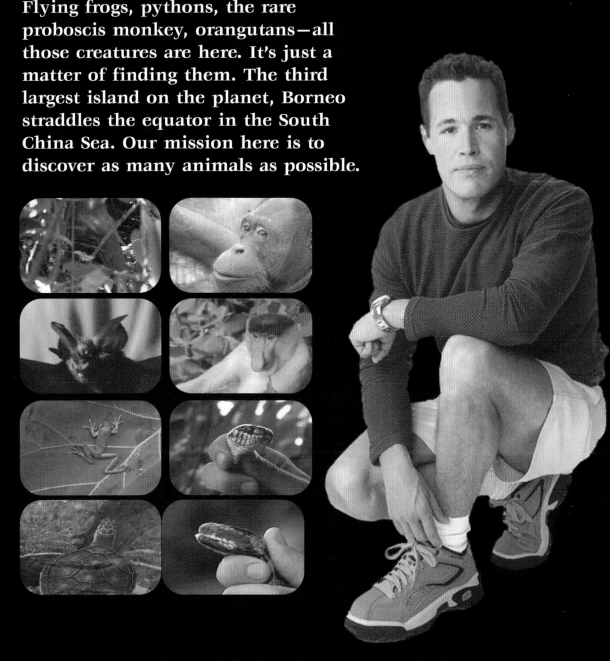

I'm Jeff Corwin.
Welcome to Borneo.

For naturalists like myself, Borneo is a great place to explore. Much of the habitat here remains pristine to this day. And because of that, Borneo is home to tons of wild animals, many of which are found nowhere else in the world.

Ahh, a naturalist's dream.

Borneo is a very dramatic island.

Heading out with Burt.

The Kinabatangan River snakes through the eastern part of Borneo. It's here that I hope to find the jungle's largest resident, the Asian elephant. I'm with Burt, a wildlife biologist who's studying a group of elephants in this area.

Tracking elephants on land.

On one side of the river we can see where this herd went into the water and swam across the river, which is 100 feet deep. Searching the other, side we discover where they came out. We've found their tracks

Elephant scat

They're in there!

and some scat. Back home we'd call something like this a road apple, but you'd probably call this a pineapple, it's so big.

I see something!

It doesn't take long to find the elephants. In fact, we are surrounded by elephants. It's amazing to me that an animal so gigantic can move so quickly through this brush and be so agile.

These are huge, powerful, and beautiful creatures.

Do you see it?

These very intelligent creatures are trumpeting to establish territory, to let us to know that they know that we are here. It's a warning. Maybe this is going to be like an elephant joke: "What do you find between an elephant's toes? Jeff Corwin."

There's a bunch of elephants in there...

...and they know I'm here.

These elephants aren't part of the main herd. They're a group of unpredictable adolescents that are off foraging on their own. They're practically invisible to us. But, occasionally, you get a glimpse of a tusk, a very brown eyeball, a long probing trunk. The elephant's trunk is extremely important. This animal uses his trunk for smelling, to pick up odor. One's doing that now, smelling me.

It's a fairly typical defensive posture for elephants to back up to their adversary. Not only can they kick their enemy, they're pretty well padded at this end.

Elephants will back up to their enemies.

For a moment it looks like we'll be able to back away from this group. But then, we stumble right into the middle of the herd. Suddenly, the jungle's filled with elephants.

We've got adults with babies forming a defensive line, and they're very angry. At this point, we are in danger. Burt tells me we have to hold our ground—but it doesn't work. Burt and I find a narrow escape route just in time.

I've seen lots of elephants in Africa, and I've seen elephants in Thailand. But I've never before encountered an elephant deep in the jungle. It was eerie, and there were times that we were really scared. But it was a thrilling experience.

Next, I'll make some new friends. Up ahead is where the road ends and our primate adventure begins. We're going to head through the bush and eventually find a wildlife sanctuary called Sepilok.

With over 10,000 acres of rain forest, Sepilok offers us the best opportunity to have a face-to-face encounter with orangutans in their natural jungle habitat.

This peaceful place is home to orangutans.

How's this for a face-to-face encounter?

See them up there?

These animals are so sensitive looking.

Not only can we encounter wild orangs, but we can meet habituated ones as well— orangs that, through a rehabilitation process, are in the process of being returned to the wild. Now, if you were a tourist you'd be limited to certain parts of the Sepilok sanctuary. But I have a permit that allows us to go off road, so we can do a little exploring.

Just ahead are two of Sepilok's treasures, a female orang and her baby. What we see is a conservation success story in the mak-

This mother and baby will go back to the wild.

ing. That female orangutan was at one time a show-piece pet, stolen from the wild and kept in a cage. When she became too hard to manage, she was left to die. Lucky for her, she was rescued and brought to Sepilok, where she is having another chance at being wild once again.

These guys have a few years before they can live on their own.

Not all of Sepilok's young have mothers. These two orphan orangs also are getting a second chance here. But it will be eight to ten years before these youngsters are ready to actually live in the wild. First they have to learn how to be wild orangs. They have to learn to climb, to find their food, to interact with other orangs.

A young orang has the strength of an adult human being. By the time it's adult, a male can grow to be 200 pounds and have the strength of up to eight men. Where is that strength? It's all in those powerful arms.

A platform within the reserve serves as a safety zone for these animals. Throughout the years that it takes them to practice, learn, and discover how to become wild again, this is where they'll come to get their food and to have some human contact.

If we go deeper into the forest, we just might find an orang that's living on its own.

These little guys are a handful!

The platform is the safety zone.

Look way up there...

There, about 35 to 40 feet up in the air, is an orangutan nest. An orang will build one of those every night, and the nests can be up as high as 60 feet. As you can see, this one is occupied. The orang is pulling in leaves and weaving them into the frame of the nest, padding it to make it comfortable.

...It's an orang nest.

Wow—there he is. He's looking at us, making noise, and shaking the branches. That's a message to us. He's saying, "I'm not afraid of you. I'm standing my ground. You are in my territory. I've picked a good place to build a nest and you're not taking over." And on that note, we'll take the message and move on.

Look inside this container. Now, this might not look like gold to you, but in Asia it's worth more than gold. This rubbery material has been harvested from the nest of a swiftlet, a bird that dwells inside caves. In Asia, it is believed that this nest, which is constructed of saliva and feathers, has many medicinal properties. And because of their rarity and the great labor it takes to harvest these nests, this stuff is extremely expensive.

Know what this is?

It's ... the swiftlet stuff.

Huge caves house the swiftlets.

In Borneo, swiftlet nests are found at the Goman-tong Caves, on the eastern coast. It's a massive cave system with a huge central grotto. And it's home not only to these birds, but to bats as well.

You don't want to trip and fall in this stuff...

Have you ever heard the saying "knee deep?" The floor of this cave, look at this, is made up of, oh, a good 8 inches of bat guano and bird guano. It's an amazing ecosystem.

These caves are teeming with life.

Everything here is a natural part of the life cycle.

The animals living above—the bats and swiftlets—feed on flying insects. Meanwhile, their guano falls to the ground, and if you look very closely you'll see there are millions of cockroaches and beetles and other insects eating the droppings. Occasionally one of the hatchling swiftlets falls to the floor, and it becomes food for the cockroaches and beetles, too. It's a little sad, and not a nice thing to see, but it is a natural part of life.

There are people here as well, and their job is to find and harvest those expensive birds' nests. Rigged up with an infrared lipstick camera, I've climbed up the tall scaffolding they use for a close look. All along the upper reaches of the caves are the birds' nests. The harvesters take the nests before the

Aha! Here's one.

birds lay their eggs, and the birds build a second set of nests in which they raise their young. Then, after the hatchlings have left, the harvesters come back and take the second nests. That way, the harvest is done in a very sustainable fashion.

Now let's go check out some bats.

Check out this face.

Bats are flying in and out of here.

To reach the bats that live in this immense cave system, we have to climb the mountain to an opening near the peak. Lots of these bats are flying in and out of a fissure in the rocks here.

I've caught one, and it's a cool-looking bat. I have to be very careful how I hold it because I really don't want to be bitten. Even with the rabies vaccination, you still don't want to be bitten—and this guy is trying to bite.

There are many things about bats that make them truly special. For one thing, they are the only mammals that are true fliers. They have special-ized wings that are made of tough skin. Inside the wings is a structure that is very similar to a human hand. Bats have long fingers that spread out and support these wings.

Another fairly unique talent of bats is using echo-location. That's an ability to navigate and find things by using sound waves. Bats send out sound waves using their mouth or nose. When the sound hits an object, an echo comes back. Bats can identify an object by the sound of the echo. They can even tell the size, shape and texture of a tiny insect from its echo.

Most bats use echolocation to navigate in the dark and find food. That's very handy, because bats live in dark caves and hunt at night.

Bats live on all continents except Antarctica. There are nearly one thousand species of these incredible mammals. They make up nearly a quarter of all animals on Earth.

You can actually see a hand inside this wing.

This is a beautiful insectivorous bat, and it's sending out a high frequency sound wave. Look at the wing—it's actually a hand. You can see its thumb and fingers. And if you look just above its nose leaf, you'll notice a crest of skin that's shaped like a horseshoe. That's why this animal is called a horseshoe bat.

Here they come...

If you're here at dusk, you get to discover a new meaning to the word "swarm." This cave exhales a great smoky cloud made up of millions of bats, spiraling out for their evening feed.

At sunrise I'm back on the river. This time, we're searching for a creature that's found only in Borneo, the reclusive proboscis monkey. I am not a morning person, but I think this is the only way we are going to successfully find this animal.

My morning monkey mission begins.

The proboscis monkey is one of the rarest primates in the world. It's got a big long muzzle and sort of a rounded belly. Actually, it looks pregnant, because it has a huge stomach filled with folds of intestine. The females have a smaller proboscis, or nose. The males have a really huge proboscis—hence the name.

I think I see something...

Check out the schnoz on this guy.

We're really surrounded by these rare creatures, moving through the branches. A male right above me just peed on my head. It doesn't get any better than that.

What I'd like to do now is find a snake. Let's continue down this river and just see what happens.

On to find some snakes.

We've found a small troupe of long-tailed macaques, and they're grooming each other.

Grooming is a very important behavior that you can see in many different types of primates. One will sit down, usually turn his back to the other one, who then commences the grooming. He just moves his finger through the hair, around the ears, all over the body, picking out any lice, ticks, or mats of dried skin.

You know, I am feeling a slightly irritating itch in a very special place. And I think I know what it is—I have become a buffet for a leech. He crawled up my leg and attached himself to a nice supply of blood.

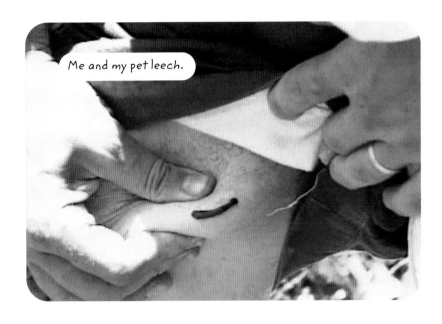

Me and my pet leech.

He will hang out there for a few more minutes and drop off. Here's a perfect example of a relationship between a parasite and a host. And, of course, I'm the host.

I'm one happy guy.

Look at that webbing.

This creature is so gorgeous.

I am extremely excited because in my hands is a frog that I've wanted to catch my entire life. This is the harlequin tree frog. Not only is it a frog that's built for living above the ground, but unlike other frogs this creature can glide. Look at his toes. Like most frogs he has webbing between his toes. But while other frogs use that webbing for swimming, this frog uses the webbing to create lift as he glides. In simple terms, his feet are like four parachutes.

Come on. I still want to find a snake.

Finally. The trick, though, is to capture this snake without being bitten. Although it's not deadly, it is venomous.

A beautiful mangrove snake.

This is a mangrove snake, and it is absolutely gorgeous. Look at those colors—beautiful bands of black and yellow. These colors are a way of warning potential predators that it is venomous. It has a diverse diet, and it'll eat everything from birds to lizards to other snakes to rodents.

His coloring is a warning to others.

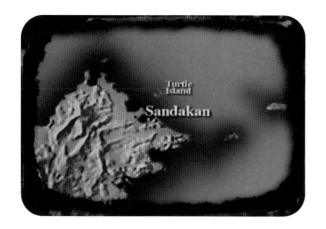

This is a special island.

These wonderful reptiles have become endangered.

Our next destination is Bakkungan Island, off the northeastern coast near the town of Sandakan. This tract of sand and palm-studded beach is extremely important to a very special group of reptiles, sea turtles. Hundreds of years ago, sea turtles would nest all over

Turtles like these can breed and nest on Bakkungan.

these islands—all over the mainland. But, because human development has taken over their habitat, these creatures have become endangered. Turtle Islands Park, which includes Bakkungan, is one of the last places on our planet where these animals can bring a new generation into the world.

Sunset in Borneo...

...and I'm waiting for the turtles to arrive.

When darkness arrives, so do the female sea turtles. They're extremely sensitive to light and sound, so we have to keep our voices and lights down so that

These swimming reptiles are so graceful in water.

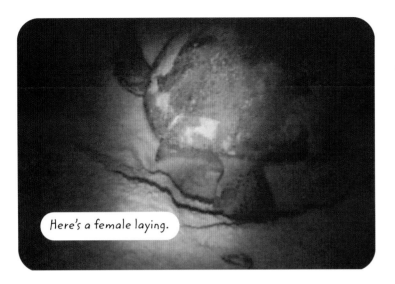

Here's a female laying.

Check out these turtle eggs.

we won't scare them off. Once the turtles start laying eggs, we don't have to worry about spooking them too much.

One of these females weighs hundreds of pounds. She pulls herself out of the ocean and up the beach using just her flippers. Then, with her back flippers, she digs a hole for her eggs. The nest cavity is about 14 to 18 inches deep. In it, she lays from 40 to 190 eggs, each about the size of a Ping-Pong ball. After she's done, she pulls sand

onto the nest, pats it down, and moves out. She's done her job, and she heads back to the ocean. She will not appear on this beach for another two or three years.

Before any predators have the chance to dig up these eggs, Chief Park Ranger Alfred Adjew and his assistant beat them to it. They take the eggs back to the island's hatchery. This stretch of sand is filled with thousands of eggs, and each nest is protected from predators by wire mesh.

We'll help these eggs stay safe.

Each of these wire things is protecting a nest.

Here's a nest that's begun to hatch.

Can you see a little pointy thing for breaking open the egg?

Is this exciting or what? The turtles in this nest have been incubating for about sixty days. And now they've started pushing their way through their eggshells. If you look on the tip if the animal's nose, you'll see there's a point that it uses to break through the shell.

The next step is to transplant the baby turtles to a bucket and count them. There are thirty two here. In the wild, less than 2 percent of these turtles would ever make it to the water. The elements or predators would claim almost all of them. With human intervention, 80 percent of the eggs can hatch. This gives many more babies a chance to survive.

As soon as they're set free, the baby turtles head for the ocean. And with some luck, in about twenty years, they'll be back to lay eggs on the beach where their lives began.

Now, the baby turtles head for the ocean.

Snake Island

Under these rocks it's teeming with snakes.

It wasn't on the schedule, but I heard about another area that is almost a legend among herpetologists. Its official name is Palaltiga, but everyone calls it Snake Island.

A fellow snake enthusiast once described this island to me. Basically, he said that coming to this place is like being a small mite in the head of Medusa—the monster in Greek myth who had snakes for hair—because all around you squirm these amazing and very venomous snakes. And to find them we're just going to look underneath the rocks where these animals like to bury themselves.

I've got a venomous sea krait here.

Look what is tucked under this rock. This beautiful creature is a yellow-lipped sea krait. These snakes are not known for being extremely aggressive, but they are very venomous—so, I'm going to handle this guy as if he's hot. And when I say hot, I mean dangerous.

This marine snake has a paddle for a tail.

Sea kraits have large, blunt heads.

Is this snake not beautiful, or what? These animals are almost completely marine. They spend 90 percent of their lives in the open ocean, swimming around coral reefs in search of eels, fish, and other animal prey. Look at that, it's a snake with a paddle. Its tail is flat and paddle shaped, giving this snake its own natural way to propel itself through the water.

Judging by the size of the snake, I think this is a she. Female sea kraits are larger than males, and this one's huge. She's about 5 feet in length, which is almost the max for these snakes. This creature produces a neurotoxin that is designed to shut down the nervous system of its prey. How powerful is that venom? Well, it is said that one teaspoon of venom from this creature is powerful enough to take out about five hundred people.

This species of snake has a large, blunt head just like its close and equally deadly relative, the cobra. Here is a male—check him out. You can see the difference between the male and the female. This guy is much smaller. I'm going to let him go.

One teaspoon of venom can kill about five hundred people...I'm being very careful.

Another amazing and exciting Borneo experience—a beautiful yellow-lipped sea krait. And I think this is a good place for us to wrap up our journey in this amazing land. We should keep in mind that animals like the ones we've discovered here, and habitats like Snake Island and the rain forest and the interior of this land, are limited resources. And, if we want them in our future, we have to begin conserving them today. Thanks for coming to Borneo!

Glossary

conservation preservation or protection

echolocation navigation by sound waves

ecosystem a community of organisms

endangered a species whose population is so low it may become extinct

fissure a crack or opening

foraging wandering and searching for food on the ground

grotto cave

guano bat droppings

habitat a place where animals and plants live naturally together

habituated returned to the wild after rehabilitation

herpetologists scientists who study reptiles and amphibians

insectivorous depending on insects for food

mammals warm-blooded animals that feeds their babies with milk

neurotoxin venom that damages the nervous system

primate a type of mammal such as monkeys, apes, or humans

pristine clean and unspoiled

rain forest a tropical forest that receives a lot of rain

rehabilitation healing and restoring strength

sanctuary a place where animals are safe and protected

scat animal droppings

venom a poison used by snakes to attack their prey or defend themselves

venomous having a gland that produces poison for self-defense or hunting

Index